Amazing Animals
Lemurs

Please visit our web site at www.garethstevens.com
For a free catalog describing our list of high-quality books, call 1-800-542-2595 (USA) or 1-800-387-3178 (Canada).
Our fax: 1-877-542-2596

Library of Congress Cataloging-in-Publication Data

Baicker, Karen.
　　Lemurs / by Karen Baicker, Kate Delaney, and Sharon Yates.
　　　　　p. cm. — (Amazing animals)
　　　　Originally published: Pleasantville, NY: Reader's Digest Young Families, copyright 2007.
　　　　Includes bibliographical references and index.
　　　　ISBN-10: 0-8368-9120-1　　　ISBN-13: 978-0-8368-9120-1 (lib. bdg.)
　　　　ISBN-10: 1-4339-2124-3　　　ISBN-13: 978-1-4339-2124-7 (soft cover)
　　　　1. Lemurs—Juvenile literature. I. Delaney, Kate. II. Yates, Sharon. III. Title.
　　QL737.P95B35 2009
　　599.8'3—dc22　　　　　　　　　　　　　　2009003926

This edition first published in 2010 by
Gareth Stevens Publishing
A Weekly Reader® Company
1 Reader's Digest Road
Pleasantville, NY 10570-7000 USA

This edition copyright © 2010 by Gareth Stevens, Inc. Original edition copyright © 2007 by Reader's Digest Young Families,
Pleasantville, NY 10570

Executive Managing Editor: Lisa M. Herrington
Senior Editor: Brian Fitzgerald
Senior Designer: Keith Plechaty

Produced by Editorial Directions, Inc.
Art Direction and Page Production: The Design Lab/Kathleen Petelinsek and Gregory Lindholm
Consultant: Robert E. Budliger (Retired), NY State Department of Environmental Conservation

Photo Credits
Front cover: Photodisc/Getty Images; title page: iStockphoto.com/Stepan Jezek; contents page: Dreamstime.com/Tze roung Tan; pages 6–7: Dreamstime.com/Lior Filshteiner; page 8: Dreamstime.com/Christian Riedel; page 11: Dreamstime.com/Wessel Cirkel; page 12: Dreamstime.com/Martina Berg; pages 14–15: Dreamstime.com; page 16: Image 100 Ltd.; page 19: Dreamstime.com/Simone Van Den Berg; page 20: Dreamstime.com/Simone Van Den Berg; page 21 (top): Dreamstime.com/Simone Van Den Berg; page 21 (bottom): Dreamstime.com/Christian Riedel; pages 22–23: iStockphoto.com/Petr Masek; page 24: iStockphoto.com/Derek Dammann; page 27: Dreamstime.com/Ben Renard-Wiart; page 28: iStockphoto.com/Peggy De Meue; page 31: iStockphoto.com; pages 32–33: David W. Kelley/Shutterstock Inc.; page 34: JupiterImages; page 35: Natalia Sinjushina & Evgeniy Meyke/Shutterstock Inc.; page 37: Simone Van Den Berg/Shutterstock Inc.; pages 38–39: Simone Van Den Berg/Shutterstock Inc.; page 43: Simone Van Den Berg/Shutterstock Inc.; pages 44–45: Laurie L. Snidow/Shutterstock Inc.; page 46: Dreamstime.com/Christian Riedel; back cover: iStockphoto.com/Stepan Jezek.

Printed in the United States of America

1 2 3 4 5 6 7 8 9 14 13 12 11 10 09

Amazing Animals
Lemurs

By Karen Baicker, Kate Delaney, and Sharon Yates

Gareth Stevens
Publishing

Contents

Chapter 1

A Lemur's Day

It is early morning on Madagascar, a big island off the coast of Africa. Streaks of sun poke through the thick, leafy treetops of the forest. A **troop** of ring-tailed lemurs is waking up after a night's sleep in the branches of a large tree. There are 12 of them in all, including sisters, cousins, aunts, and a few grown-up males.

The baby lemur is not really a baby anymore. He is two months old and much bigger than when he was born. He still likes to snuggle at night with his mother for warmth. He also needs to hitch rides with her when the troop moves through the treetops.

After eating some fruit for breakfast, the young lemurs play among the tangle of vines and branches. They jump and hide as the sun casts shadows through the leaves.

After a while, the mother gives a few short calls to the troop. "*Mew! Mew! Mew!*" The lemurs know she is telling them to follow her. The baby scampers onto his mother's back and holds on tightly. The mother moves down the tree backward. She goes tail first, and the others climb down after her.

Forest Ghosts

When early explorers saw these animals with their glow-in-the-dark eyes and eerie sounds, they thought the creatures could be ghosts. The explorers called the animals *lemurs* (LEE-merz), a term based on the Latin word for "ghosts."

The tropical dry forest in this part of the island has patches of open land among the trees. This is where the troop likes to sunbathe. The lemurs lie on the ground or against a tree. They stretch out to soak up the warm sun.

Soon one of the baby's cousins comes over to groom his hair. She uses her bottom teeth for a comb, catching seeds and dirt and smoothing his matted fur. The other lemurs begin to groom one another, too. It doesn't matter who is old or young, a leader or a follower. They all groom one another.

"*Click! Click!*" The mother is telling her troop that it is time to look for food. She leads the way, with her baby hanging onto her back. The males follow along behind the females and young lemurs. They make a funny-looking parade, walking on all fours with their tails up in the air.

The male lemurs give the mother some seedpods from a tamarind tree. She cracks the tough pods open with her sharp teeth. Then she shares the treat with her baby. The flesh inside the pods tastes bitter and sour.

Now it is time to look for food in the treetops. Off the troop goes, leaping from branch to branch and tree to tree. They soar like acrobats 100 feet (30 meters) above the ground. Their long, bushy tails wave in the air, helping them keep their balance.

The Island of Madagascar

Madagascar is an island in the Indian Ocean, 250 miles (402 kilometers) off the coast of eastern Africa. It is the fourth-largest island in the world. It has many different **habitats**. The southwestern part of the island has tropical dry forests. The climate is warm, and there is very little rain. Ring-tailed lemurs live in these forests.

The mother finds a ripe bunch of fruit hanging from a tree. She makes sure that her baby gets the ripest, sweetest fruit. Just then, another troop of ring-tailed lemurs comes along. They want to eat there, too. Oops! Whose **territory** is it?

The baby senses a fight coming on! He is right. Quickly, his troop climbs down to the ground. One of his male cousins faces a member of the other troop. They are glaring at each other and shifting their bodies around. Both rub their tails just above their wrists. This movement picks up a scent the lemurs release from their bodies. They wave their tails in the air, spreading their strong smells. It's a stink fight! The other males join in. The female lemurs jump and scream their support. The baby's troop has the more powerful smell. The other troop leaves. This territory now belongs to the baby's troop.

The lemurs go back to playing and relaxing. When the sun begins to set, they climb to the safety of the treetops to spend the night. Up high, they can watch out for **predators**, such as hawks, eagles, other lemurs, and the catlike fossas. The fossas are the largest hunters on the island.

Now the baby snuggles close to his mother's belly. He wraps his tail around himself for greater warmth. Then his mother wraps her tail around the two of them. The baby's family is all around him, and he is safe.

Chapter 2
The Body of a Lemur

15

Lemurs have large eyes and pointy noses. Their "hands" and "feet" are shaped for grasping objects.

What Is a Lemur?

A lemur is a small, fur-covered **mammal** with four legs. It looks a bit like a monkey. It has very big eyes, a long, pointy **snout**, and long "fingers" and "toes." Almost all lemurs have an extra-long, furry tail. All lemurs in the wild live on Madagascar and the nearby tiny islands of Comoros.

There are many different types of lemurs. Some have reddish brown fur. Others are shades of brown, gray, or black. A few are black and white. Some have a **ruff** of fur around their heads. Lemurs can be as small as mice or as big as house cats.

Lemurs Are Primates

Lemurs are members of a big group of animals called **primates.** Primates also include monkeys, gorillas, chimpanzees, and humans. Primates have large brains compared to the size of their bodies. They can use their hands to grasp things because they have **opposable** thumbs, just like humans do.

Some primates, such as lemurs, have been on Earth longer than other primates. They are **prosimians** (pro-SIM-ee-unz), which means "coming before monkeys and apes." Unlike monkeys and apes, though, prosimians can't use their hands well, and their brains are small.

Glow-in-the-Dark Eyes

Lemurs have very big, round eyes that face forward. This position allows lemurs to judge how close objects are. That judgment is important when leaping from tree to tree.

Big eyes let in more light, giving lemurs excellent night vision. Many kinds of lemurs, especially the smaller ones, are active at night. That is when fewer predators are out looking for their next meal. Lemur eyes seem to glow like cat eyes do. In the daytime, their eyes seem to pop right out of their heads!

Super Snouts

Lemur noses are moist, have no fur, and stick out far from their faces. Lemurs have a super sense of smell. They can smell a piece of fruit buried under a pile of leaves or know if another lemur has been on the same branch— just by sniffing. Lemurs use smells to communicate with one another and for defense against other lemurs.

Thumb-Thing Special

Like all primates, lemurs have opposable thumbs and big toes. This lets lemurs grasp and pick up objects. Unlike monkeys, chimps, gorillas, and humans, lemurs usually keep their fingers and toes together when they use them. This gives them less control. Try unbuttoning your coat while wearing mittens, and you'll see the difference.

Lemur eyes seem to glow both at night and in the daytime!

The sifaka (suh-FAH-ka) is a type of lemur. It can leap to a tree or branch 30 feet (9 m) away, about the length of a school bus.

Long Legs

Most lemurs have long, strong back legs. Their legs give them great power for running and leaping. Many lemurs jump from branch to branch and tree to tree. Some lemurs jump in a standing position. They look like they are flying! The bottoms of lemur feet are padded, which helps to soften landings.

A Tall Tail

Most lemurs have long, fur-covered tails. A ring-tailed lemur's tail is about 25 inches (64 centimeters) long. That is about 7 inches (18 cm) longer than its body. Unlike monkeys, lemurs cannot hang from their tails. Lemurs use their tails for balance as they move from tree to tree. Some lemurs raise their tails high to tell other members of their group where they are. The ring-tailed lemur uses its tail as a very smelly weapon to make predators and other lemurs go away.

Chapter 3
Lemur Life

Members of a lemur troop spend lots of time together—eating, resting, and grooming one another.

Group Life

Most lemurs live together in groups. Some kinds of lemurs live in a family troop that has one female, one male, and their children. Others live in larger groups. Still others form big troops of 30 or more.

Adult females lead the troops. They decide how the lemurs in their group spend the day. They also decide where the troop will go to find food and to rest. Within a troop, some lemurs are more important and have more power than others. The higher-ranked members get the best food and places to sleep.

When a troop takes its midday break, the lemurs groom one another. During grooming, the **status** of each lemur does not matter. They all pick bugs out of one another's fur!

Combs and Toothbrushes

Lemurs have built-in tooth combs and toothbrushes that they use to clean one another's fur. Their lower front teeth are flat and are lined up like the teeth of hair combs. The lemurs clean their fur with their teeth the way we use combs in our hair. Lemurs also have something like a brush under their tongues for cleaning out the bits and pieces from the tooth combs.

Lemur Screamers

Lemurs are very noisy creatures! Different kinds of lemurs make different sounds. These sounds range from soft hums to screeches and howls. Each kind of sound has a different meaning.

A soft hum tells lemurs the troop is ready to move to a new location. A loud chorus of shrieks warns other creatures to back off. Troops of indri lemurs "sing" to one another in the forest several times a day, using eerie, wailing sounds. This may be how they stay in contact or announce the location of their territory.

Yelps, screeches, and howls warn other lemurs of danger. The indri lemur makes a loud barking noise when the predator is a bird of prey like an eagle or hawk. When the predator is an animal that moves on the ground, the indri hoots. When another lemur hears these sounds, it knows it should find a safe place to hide.

Sniffing Around

Lemurs also use smells to communicate. Lemurs release different kinds of scents to send different messages. Ring-tailed lemurs smear a really stinky scent on their tails. Then they wave their tails in the air to chase off predators and other lemurs. Another way lemurs use their scents is to mark territories as their own.

Smells That Tell

Each lemur has a unique smell. Members of a troop can identify one another by smell alone!

For such small animals, lemurs can make very loud noises. Some howls can be heard 2 miles (3 km) away!

Lemurs can pick up the smell of ripe fruit from very far away. They enjoy some of the same fruit that you do!

Favorite Foods

Most lemurs are plant eaters. They eat flowers, fruit, and leaves. Some lemurs also eat insects and other small animals.

The favorite food of most lemurs is fruit, such as bananas and figs. Lemurs use their fingers to pull branches close to their mouths. Then they use their sharp front teeth to bite off fruit. When lemurs are thirsty, they lick the dew off leaves or drink water from streams.

From October to April, the rainy season provides plenty of food. In May, the dry season begins. For the next few months, there is very little rain. Food is scarce. Lemurs survive by living off their own fat and eating other things, such as tree bark.

Keep Out!

Some lemurs stay in one main area, called their home **range**. They claim a territory as their own. The troop settles in an area where there will be enough food for them. They mark the territory with their own scents. If other lemurs have tried to claim the same territory, the new lemurs may try to out-stink the lemurs that were there before. The new lemurs rub their smell over the first smell. Whichever troop has the worst stink wins!

Mothers and Babies

Lemur babies are born in the early fall, often in a nest. Usually a female lemur gives birth to just one or two babies at a time. For the first three weeks, mother mouse lemurs carry their babies from place to place in their mouths. Baby indri lemurs sleep with their moms every night for a whole year. They like being safely cuddled inside the curve of their mothers' bodies.

Baby ring-tailed lemurs cling to the stomachs of their mothers for a few weeks. Then they climb on their mothers' backs and ride piggyback style. At about six weeks old, the baby ring-tailed lemurs become bold. They hop down to the ground for a few seconds at a time. Gradually, the little lemurs spend more time on their own. The whole troop helps to raise the young lemurs until they are two years old. Then they can survive as adults.

The Aye-Aye

The aye-aye is another interesting primate that lives on Madagascar. It is one of the world's strangest-looking animals. With bat-like ears and glowing orange eyes, the aye-aye looks like an alien creature. The aye-aye is about the size of a cat. It has huge, sharp front teeth. Its long, bony fingers and toes are twisted and end in still-longer curved nails.

Aye-ayes sleep during the day and climb among the trees at night. The aye-aye is hardly ever seen. It is thought to be almost extinct.

Ring-tailed lemur babies blend in perfectly with their moms when they ride on their backs.

Chapter 4
Kinds of Lemurs

Sifakas leap from one tree trunk to another in an upright position. They often land by wrapping both their front and back legs around the trunk.

The Sifaka

There are more than 40 different kinds of lemurs. Scientists continue to discover more of them. Each kind of lemur is special in its own way.

The long-legged sifaka is one of the most fascinating of all lemurs. Whether eating, sleeping, or traveling, sifakas spend most of their time high in the treetops. When these excellent leapers must travel on the ground, they can't walk on all fours. Their hind legs are much longer than their front legs. This throws them off balance. So they bound along upright on their hind legs. The movement is a strange sideways dance, legs together, and arms waving in the air. They look like a group of clumsy ballet dancers!

Small Stuff

The tiny mouse lemur is so small that you could hold it on your finger. The huge, round eyes of the mouse lemur help it see well at night. This is helpful as it leaps from branch to branch in search of food. Even though mouse lemurs are tiny, they can leap across a 10-foot (3 m) span. When food is scarce, they live off fat that they have stored in their tails.

The Indri

The indri lemur is the largest of all the lemurs. Unlike other lemurs, which have long tails, the indri has a little, stumpy tail.

Even with no tail to help with balance, the indri is an excellent leaper. It comfortably jumps from tree to tree, usually landing upright on its hind legs. It seldom leaves the leafy top of the forest except to cross small areas that have no trees.

Indris live in small family groups made up of a male, a female, and their youngsters. A baby indri stays close to its mother for almost a year before it leaves her side.

The Ring-tailed Lemur

The ring-tailed lemur spends more time on the ground than any other lemur. It walks on all four legs, with its tail high in the air.

Ring-tailed lemurs use their tails to keep track of one another as they look for food. The males also use them as smelly weapons! Males have **glands** just above their wrists that produce a strong odor. When threatened, the male lemurs rub their tails over the glands. Then they wave their tails—and their stink—in the direction of the intruders. Who wins? The lemurs with the smelliest stink!

The large indri doesn't "pick" the fruit and leaves it eats. Instead, it eats them directly from a tree's branches.

Chapter 5
Lemurs in the World

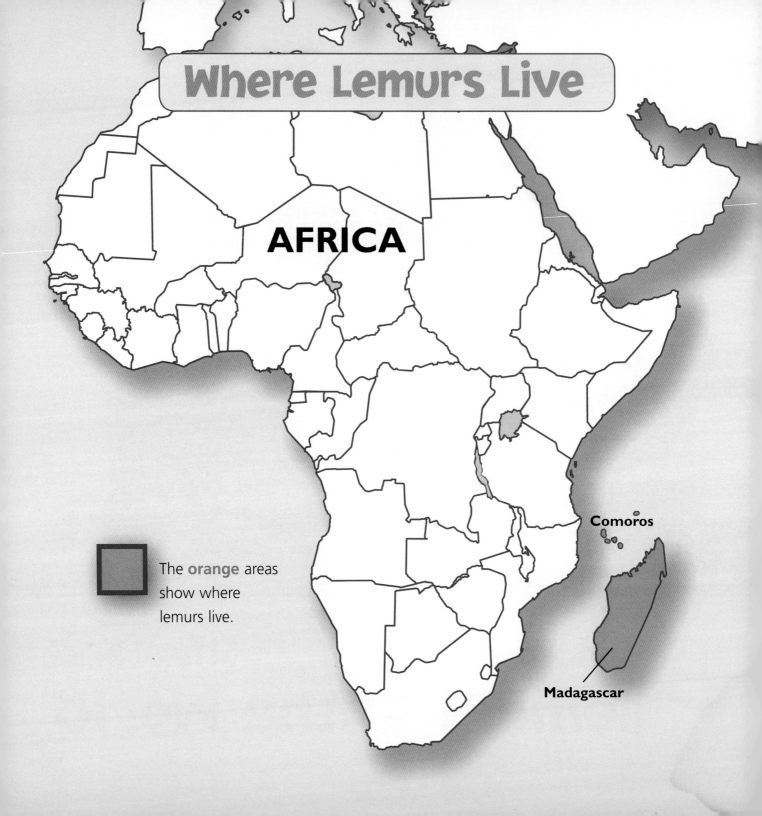

Where Lemurs Live

AFRICA

The **orange** areas show where lemurs live.

Comoros

Madagascar

Island Dwellers

Lemurs in the wild live only on the island of Madagascar and the tiny Comoros islands in the Indian Ocean. Madagascar has many different habitats. These include seashores, dry forests, rain forests, deserts, and mountains. Madagascar was once part of Africa. Millions of years ago, before lemurs existed, it broke off and drifted away. So how did lemurs get to the island?

Nature's Rafts

Scientists believe that the ancient relatives of modern lemurs floated to Madagascar on logs and clumps of plants and dirt. Once on the island, the lemurs were safe because large predators were too heavy to survive the same journey. The island lemurs multiplied into many different types. The lemurs that stayed in Africa died out because stronger and smarter animals killed them. Humans arrived on Madagascar about 2,000 years ago. That's when trouble began for the lemurs. The lemurs were hunted, and their forest homes were cut down to make room for people's homes and farms. Most of the original rain forests are gone. Today about 18 million people live on Madagascar.

The Red Island

Madagascar is sometimes called the Red Island because of the color of its soil. Madagascar is the fourth-largest island in the world. This island is bigger than California.

Saving the Lemurs

Lemurs have a few natural predators, such as snakes, hawks, eagles, and fossas. However, the biggest threat comes from people. Many lemurs are in danger of extinction because so many trees have been cut down. Without trees, lemurs have no place to live.

Many people want to save the lemurs. Areas on Madagascar are being set aside for lemurs, and there are efforts to save the forests. Islanders who used to make money by cutting down and selling trees can instead work in the tourist industry. Madagascar is encouraging tourism that observes and helps protect nature.

Fast Facts About Ring-Tailed Lemurs

Scientific name	*Lemur catta*
Class	Mammals
Order	Primates
Size	Body: up to 18 inches (46 cm)
	Tail: about 25 inches (64 cm)
Weight	Up to 8 pounds (4 kg)
Life span	20–25 years
Habitat	Tropical dry forests

At the Primate Center at Duke University in North Carolina, scientists raise lemurs. When the lemurs are old enough to survive on their own, they are taken to the forests of Madagascar and released.

Glossary

canopy—a covering of large, leafy treetops, like a roof, over a forest

gland—a part of the body that makes chemicals and often releases them, sometimes as a scent

habitat—the natural environment where an animal or plant lives

mammal—a kind of animal with a backbone and hair on its body; it drinks milk from its mother when it is born

opposable—describing a thumb on a hand (or foot) that is opposite other fingers (or toes), allowing the animal to grasp objects

predator—an animal that hunts and eats other animals to survive

primate—a mammal with a large brain and complex hands and feet

prosimian—a kind of animal that developed before monkeys and apes and is not as advanced

range—all the places where a plant or animal lives

ruff—a band of fur around an animal's neck and sometimes around its face

snout—the part of an animal's head where the nose and jaws stick out

status—rank or social position in a group

territory—an area of land that an animal considers to be its own and will fight to defend

troop—a group of animals that live together

Lemurs: Show What You Know

How much have you learned about lemurs? Grab a piece of paper and a pencil and write your answers down.

1. When early explorers first saw lemurs, what did they think the creatures were?

2. What are some predators that lemurs have to look out for?

3. How long is a ring-tailed lemur's tail?

4. In the wild, where do wild lemurs live?

5. What do lemurs use to clean their fur?

6. What is a way lemurs can communicate without using sounds?

7. What is the favorite food of most lemurs?

8. How many different kinds of lemurs are there?

9. What kind of lemur has a short, stumpy tail?

10. What is the biggest threat to lemurs?

1. Ghosts 2. Hawks, eagles, snakes, fossas, and other lemurs 3. About 25 inches (64 cm)
4. On Madagascar and the Comoros Islands. 5. Their comb-like teeth 6. They can use
different scents. 7. Fruit 8. More than 40, and scientists are discovering more 9. The indri
10. Humans destroying their habitat

For More Information

Books

Buckingham, Suzanne. *Meet the Ring-Tailed Lemur.* New York: PowerKids Press, 2008.

Heale, Jay, and Zawiah Abdul Latif. *Madagascar* (Cultures of the World). Tarrytown, NY: Marshall Cavendish Children's Books, 2008.

Riley, Joelle. *Ring-Tailed Lemurs* (Early Bird Nature Books). Minneapolis: Lerner Publications, 2009.

Web Sites

Animal Planet: Lemur

http://animal.discovery.com/mammals/lemur

Learn about the different species of lemurs, view great photos, and find out about threats to lemurs today.

National Geographic Kids: Ring-Tailed Lemurs

http://kids.nationalgeographic.com/Animals/CreatureFeature/Ring-tailed-lemur

Get quick facts and photos of the ring-tailed lemur.

Publisher's note to educators and parents: Our editors have carefully reviewed these web sites to ensure that they are suitable for children. Many web sites change frequently, however, and we cannot guarantee that a site's future contents will continue to meet our high standards of quality and educational value. Be advised that children should be closely supervised whenever they access the Internet.

Index